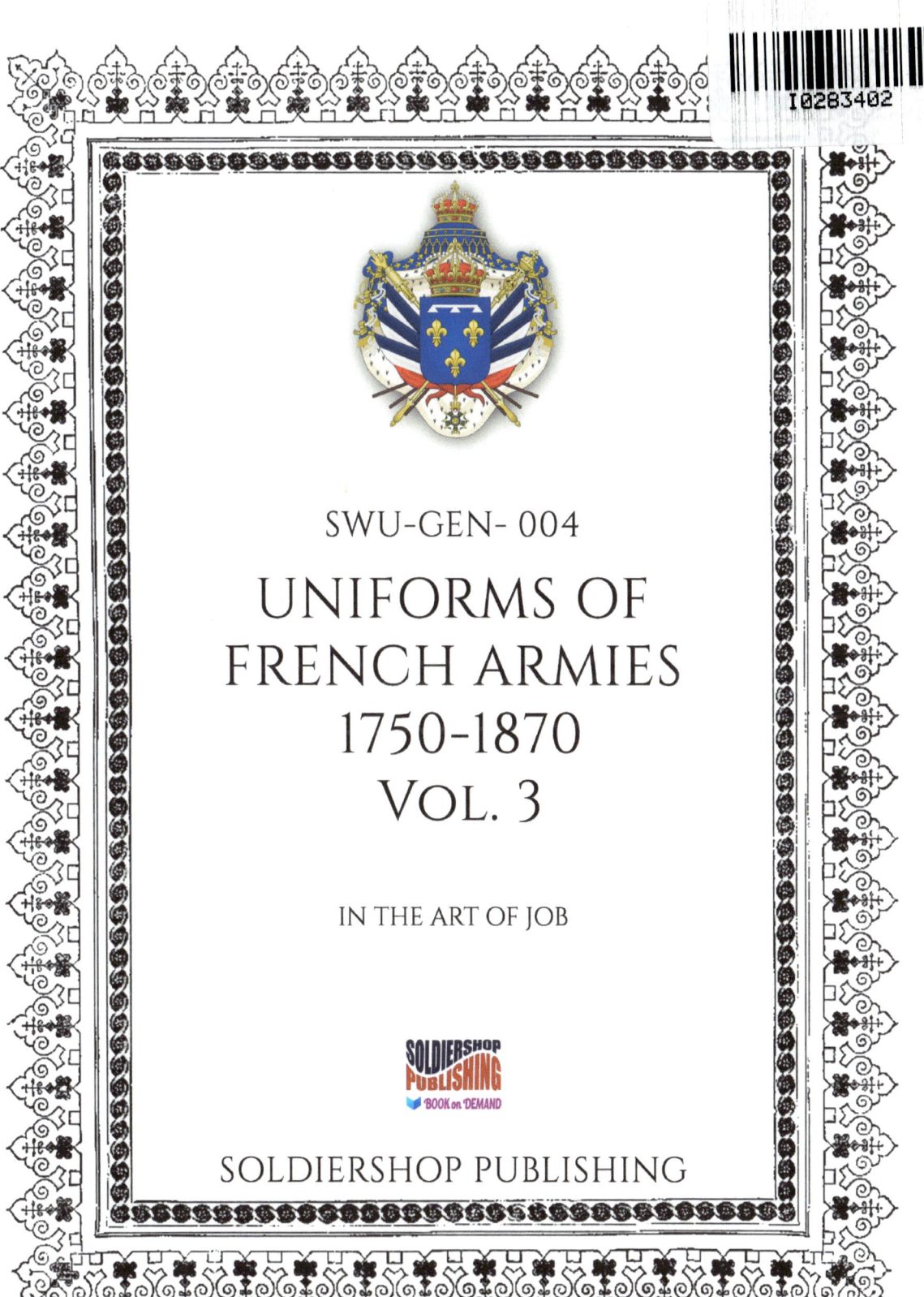

SWU-GEN- 004

UNIFORMS OF FRENCH ARMIES 1750-1870 VOL. 3

IN THE ART OF JOB

SOLDIERSHOP PUBLISHING

AUTHOR
Jacques Marie Gaston Onfroy de Bréville, known by the pen name **Job** after his initials (25 November 1858, Bar-le-Duc – 15 September 1931, Neuilly-sur-Seine) was a famous French artist and illustrator that maintained a keen taste for military, patriotic and nationalistic subjects.

PUBLISHING'S NOTE
None of **unpublished** images or text of our book may be reproduced in any format without the expressed written permission of Soldiershop.com when not indicate as marked with license creative commons 3.0 or 4.0. The publisher remains to disposition of the possible having right for all the doubtful sources images or not identifies. Our trademark: Soldiershop Publishing ©, The names of our series: Soldiers&Weapons, Battlefield, War in colour, PaperSoldiers, Soldiershop e-book etc. are herein © by Soldiershop.com.

NOTE ABOUT BOOK PRINTING BEFORE 1925
This book may contain text or images coming from a reproduction of a book published before 1925 (over seventy years ago). No effort has been made to modernize or standardize the spelling used in the original text, so this book may have occasional imperfections such as missing or blurred pages, poor pictures, errant marks, etc. that were either part of the original artifact, or were introduced by the scanning process. We believe this work is culturally important, and despite the imperfections, have elected to bring it back into print (digital and/or paper) as part of our continuing commitment to the preservation of printed works worldwide. We appreciate your understanding of the imperfections in the preservation process, and hope you enjoy this valuable book. Now this book is purpose re-built and is proof-read and re-type set from the original to provide an outstanding experience of reflowing text, also for an ebook reader. However Soldiershop publishing added, enriched, revised and overhauled the text, images, etc. of the cover and the book. Therefore, the job is now to all intents and purposes a derivative work, and the added, new and original parts of the book are the copyright of Soldiershop. On this second unpublished part of the book none of images or text may be reproduced in any format without the expressed written permission of Soldiershop. Almost many of the images of our books and prints are taken from original first edition prints or books that are no longer in copyright and are therefore public domain. We have been a specialized bookstore for a long time so we (and several friends antiquarian booksellers) have readily available a lot of ancient, historical and illustrated books not in copyright. Each of our prints, art designs or illustrations is either our own creation, or a fully digitally restoration by our computer artists, or non copyrighted images. All of our prints are "tagged" with a registered digital copyright. Soldiershop remains to disposition of the possible having right for all the doubtful sources images or not identifies.

LICENSES COMMONS
Much of the text in this book are from the *"Memoirs of the Empress Catherine II., by Catherine II, Empress of Russia"* This book is for the use of anyone anywhere at no cost and with almost no restrictions whatsoever. You may copy it, give it away or re-use it under the terms of the similar creative commons License. This book may utilize material marked with license creative commons 3.0 or 4.0 (CC BY 4.0), (CC BY-ND 4.0), (CC BY-SA 4.0) or (CC0 1.0). We give appropriate attribution credit and indicate if change were made below in the acknowledgements field.

ACKNOWLEDGEMENTS
A Special Thanks to NYPL and other institutions for their kindly permission to use some images of his archives, collections or books used in our book.

Title: **UNIFORMS OF FRENCH ARMIES 1750-1870 VOL. 3** - The French soldiers in the XIX century - In the art of Job
By Luca Stefano Cristini, color plates by Job. Serie edit by Luca S. Cristini. First edition by Soldiershop. July 2019
Cover & Art Design: Luca S. Cristini. ISBN code: 978-88-93274364
Published by Luca Cristini Editore, via Orio 35/4- 24050 Zanica (BG) ITALY. www.soldiershop.com

UNIFORMS OF FRENCH ARMIES 1750-1870 Vol. 3

THE FRENCH SOLDIERS IN THE XIX CENTURY IN THE ART OF JOB

Luca Stefano Cristini

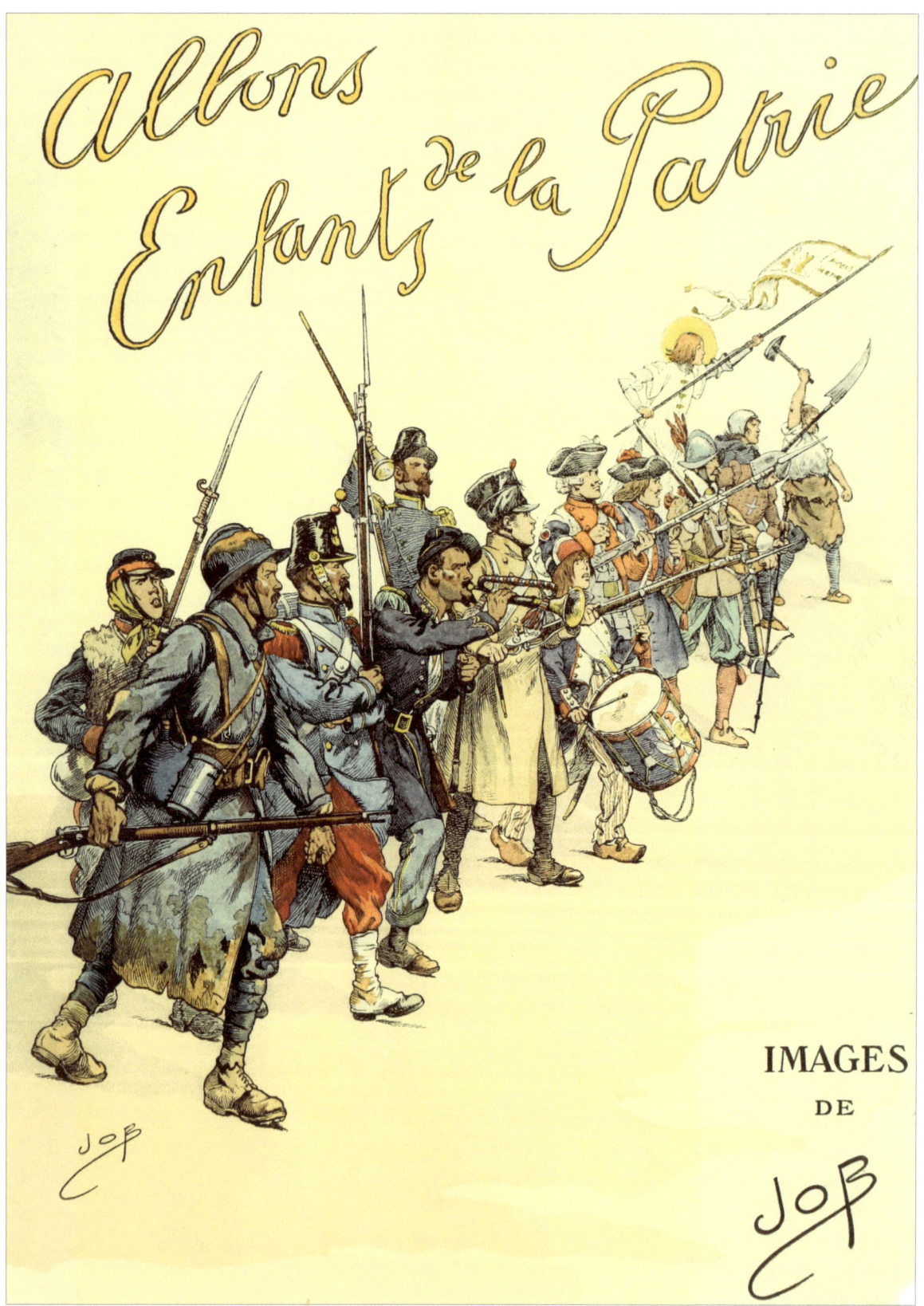

THE WONDERFUL WORLD OF THE JOB'S SOLDIERS

In this book are present the development and complexity of France's uniforms, from the Louis XV era just to Second Empire of Napoleon III. All the subjects are seen through the eyes of a great French artist. Jacques Marie Gaston Onfroy de Bréville, well known by the pen name Job after his initials (1858-1931).
The serie is published on 3 volume that includes about 200 and more wonderful original illustrations of uniforms from the 18th century to Napoleonic era and just to 1870 about.
This book presents pictorial documentation of the appearance of French soldiers throughout the period with the support of short essays on France's military history. The particularly well-executed original Job's illustrations, slightly restored by our graphic artist are presented to the general public here for the first time. Job's plates shows how the Royal and (after) Imperial French Army, time and again, was a decisive factor in the story of Europe.

In the 3rd volume of the serie we present the French soldiers during the years of XIX century.

IL MERAVIGLIOSO MONDO DEI SOLDATI DI JOB

In questo libro presentiamo il fascino e la storia delle uniformi francesi, dalle armate di Luigi XV a Napoleone III e il Secondo Impero. Tutti soggetti sono opera di un solo grande artista: Jacques Marie Gaston Onfroy de Bréville (1858-1931), meglio noto con lo pseudonimo di Job, dalle iniziali del suo nome. Tutte le tavole fanno parte di una collezione di oltre duecento disegni a colori, e sono presentati su tre volumi. Si tratta come è noto del periodo più glorioso della storia di Francia, e la maestria di Job, fervente patriota oltre che grande artista, rende particolare merito a queste tavole capolavoro. Questo lavoro è anche il primo mai edito in Italia.
In questo terzo volume sono trattate le uniformi dalla fine dell'era napoleonica fino al crollo del secondo impero. Buona lettura e soprattutto buona visione

Portrait of Louis Philippe, King of France (1830-1848) paint by Franz Xaver Winterhalter, 1841

SHORT HISTORY OF THE FRENCH ARMY

THE FRENCH SOLDIER IN THE XIX CENTURY

After the exile of Napoleon, the freshly restored Bourbon monarchy helped the absolute Bourbon king of Spain to recover his throne during the French intervention in Spain. To restore the prestige of the French monarchy, disputed by the Revolution and the First Empire, Charles X engaged in the military conquest of Algeria in 1830. This marked the beginning of a new expansion of the French colonial empire throughout the 19th century. In that century, France remained a major force in continental affairs. After the July Revolution, the liberal king Louis Philippe I victoriously supported the Spanish and Belgian liberals. The French later inflicted a defeat on the Habsburgs in the Franco-Austrian War of 1859, a victory which led to the unification of Italy in 1861, after having triumphed over Russia with other allies in the Crimean War. Detrimentally, however, the French army emerged from these victories in an overconfident and complacent state. France's defeat in the Franco-Prussian War led to the loss of Alsace-Lorraine and the creation of a united German Empire, both results representing major failures in long-term French foreign policy and sparking a vengeful, nationalist revanchism meant to earn back former territories. The Dreyfus Affair, however, mitigated these nationalist tendencies by prompting public skepticism about the competence of the military.

French colonial empire

The history of French colonial imperialism can be divided in two major eras: the first from the early 17th century to the middle of the 18th century, and the second from the early 19th century to the middle of the 20th century. In the first phase of expansion, France concentrated its efforts mainly in North America, the Caribbean and India, setting up commercial ventures that were backed by military force. Following defeat in the Seven Years' War, France lost its possessions in North America and India, but it did manage to keep the wealthy Caribbean islands of Saint-Domingue, Guadeloupe, and Martinique.
The second stage began with the conquest of Algeria in 1830, then with the establishment of French Indochina (covering modern Vietnam, Laos, and Cambodia) and a string of military victories in the Scramble for Africa, where it established control over regions covering much of West Africa, Central Africa and Maghreb. In 1914 France had an empire stretching over 13,000,000 km² (6,000,000 mile²) of land and about 110 million people. [52] Following victory in World War I, Togo and most of Cameroon were also added to the French possessions, and Syria and Lebanon became French mandates. For most of the period from 1870 to 1945, France was territorially the third largest nation on Earth, after Britain and Russia (later the Soviet Union), and had the most overseas possessions following Britain. Following the Second World War, France struggled to preserve French territories but wound up losing the First Indochina War (the precursor to the Vietnam War) and granting independence to Algeria after a long war. Today, France still maintains a number of overseas territories, but their collective size is barely a shadow of the old French colonial empire.

The Franco-Prussian War or Franco-German War

Often referred to in France as the War of 1870, was a conflict between the Second French Empire and later the Third French Republic, and the German states of the North German Confederation led by the Kingdom of Prussia. Lasting from 19 July 1870 to 28 January 1871, the conflict was caused by Prussian ambitions to extend German unification and French fears of the shift in the European balance of power that would result if the Prussians succeeded. Some historians argue that the Prussian chancellor Otto von Bismarck deliberately provoked the French into declaring war on Prussia in order to draw the independent southern German states—

Baden, Württemberg, Bavaria and Hesse-Darmstadt—into an alliance with the North German Confederation dominated by Prussia, while others contend that Bismarck did not plan anything and merely exploited the circumstances as they unfolded. None, however, dispute the fact that Bismarck must have recognized the potential for new German alliances, given the situation as a whole. On 16 July 1870, the French parliament voted to declare war on Prussia and hostilities began three days later when French forces invaded German territory. The German coalition mobilised its troops much more quickly than the French and rapidly invaded northeastern France. The German forces were superior in numbers, had better training and leadership and made more effective use of modern technology, particularly railroads and artillery.

A series of swift Prussian and German victories in eastern France, culminating in the Siege of Metz and the Battle of Sedan, saw French Emperor Napoleon III captured and the army of the Second Empire decisively defeated. A Government of National Defence declared the Third French Republic in Paris on 4 September and continued the war for another five months; the German forces fought and defeated new French armies in northern France. Following the Siege of Paris, the capital fell on 28 January 1871, and then a revolutionary uprising called the Paris Commune seized power in the city and held it for two months, until it was bloodily suppressed by the regular French army at the end of May 1871.

The German states proclaimed their union as the German Empire under the Prussian king Wilhelm I, finally uniting Germany as a nation-state. The Treaty of Frankfurt of 10 May 1871 gave Germany most of Alsace and some parts of Lorraine, which became the Imperial territory of Alsace-Lorraine (*Reichsland Elsaß-Lothringen*). The German conquest of France and the unification of Germany upset the European balance of power that had existed since the Congress of Vienna in 1815, and Otto von Bismarck maintained great authority in international affairs for two decades.

French determination to regain Alsace-Lorraine and fear of another Franco-German war, along with British apprehension about the balance of power, became factors in the causes of World War I

The French army during the second empire

The French Army consisted in peacetime of approximately 400,000 soldiers, some of them regulars, others conscripts who until 1869 served the comparatively long period of seven years with the colours. Some of them were veterans of previous French campaigns in the Crimean War, Algeria, the Franco-Austrian War in Italy, and in the Mexican campaign. However, following the "Seven Weeks War" between Prussia and Austria four years earlier, it had been calculated that the French Army could field only 288,000 men to face the Prussian Army when potentially 1,000,000 would be required. Under Marshal Adolphe Niel, urgent reforms were made. Universal conscription (rather than by ballot, as previously) and a shorter period of service gave increased numbers of reservists, who would swell the army to a planned strength of 800,000 on mobilisation. Those who for any reason were not conscripted were to be enrolled in the *Garde Mobile*, a militia with a nominal strength of 400,000. However, the Franco-Prussian War broke out before these reforms could be completely implemented. The mobilisation of reservists was chaotic and

Napoleon III portrait by F. Winterhalter

resulted in large numbers of stragglers, while the *Garde Mobile* were generally untrained and often mutinous. French infantry were equipped with the breech-loading Chassepot rifle, one of the most modern mass-produced firearms in the world at the time. With a rubber ring seal and a smaller bullet, the Chassepot had a maximum effective range of some 1,500 metres (4,900 ft) with a short reloading time. French tactics emphasised the defensive use of the Chassepot rifle in trench-warfare style fighting—the so-called *feu de bataillon*. The artillery was equipped with rifled, muzzle-loaded La Hitte guns. The army also possessed a precursor to the machine-gun: the mitrailleuse, which could unleash significant, concentrated firepower but nevertheless lacked range and was comparatively immobile, and thus prone to being easily overrun. The mitrailleuse was mounted on an artillery gun carriage and grouped in batteries in a similar fashion to cannon.

The army was nominally led by Napoleon III, with Marshals Francois Achille Bazaine and Patrice de Mac-Mahon in command of the field armies. However, there was no previously arranged plan of campaign in place. The only campaign plan prepared between 1866 and 1870 was a defensive one.

THE ARTIS JOB

Jacques Marie Gaston Onfroy de Bréville, known by the pen name **Job** after his initials (25 November 1858, Bar-le-Duc – 15 September 1931, Neuilly-sur-Seine) was a French artist and illustrator. His father opposed his entry to thé École des beaux-arts after graduating from the Collège Stanislas. He therefore joined the French army, but returned to Paris in 1882. In the intervening period, he maintained a keen taste for military, patriotic and nationalistic subjects. He finally joined the École des beaux-arts and exhibited at the 1886 'Salon des artistes français', receiving a mixed reception. He therefore began a career as an illustrator, contributing caricatures to *La Caricature* and to *La Lune*. However, he is best known for his illustrations for children's books, most frequently for texts by Georges Montorgueil. His major colour compositions contributed to the cult of 'heroes of the nation' such as Napoleon I and Joachim Murat. Several of his illustrations appear in *La Vieille Garde impériale*

Job pencil self portrait

(*The Old Imperial Guard*), published in 1932 by Alfred Mame and fils de Tours. His eye for detail can be seen in *L'Épopée du costume militaire français* - even in works intended for children, he tried to reproduce uniforms with extreme precision.

His best known works are *Murat, Le Grand Napoléon des petits enfants, Jouons à l'histoire, Louis XI, Napoléon, Bonaparte* and *Les Gourmandises de Charlotte*. He also illustrated the life of George Washington and was well known in the USA. He was a Sociétaire of the 'humoristes' and exhibited with the Incoherents. His studio has been reconstructed at the musée de Metz

Young and oldest French soldiers by Job.

THE PLATES
Vol. 3

GROUPE D'OFFICIERS D'ARTILLERIE DE LA GARDE IMPÉRIALE (1813)
(D'après un tableau de de Lassus).

1813 Officers and trumpet of the horse artillery guard

1813 Cuirassier marshall of Logis, 7th Regt.

TAMBOUR-MAITRE D'INFANTERIE LÉGÈRE

EN GRANDE TENUE

GRENADIER D'INFANTERIE

1813 Tambour de light infantry and infantry grenadier

TROMPETTE ET SOUS-ADJUDANT MAJOR DE L'ARTILLERIE A CHEVAL DE LA GARDE IMPÉRIALE (1813)
(D'après un tableau de de Lassus).

1813 Trumpet and subwarrant Officer major of the horse Artillery of the Imperial Guard

CUIRASSIERS A PIED DU 1ᵉʳ RÉGIMENT, FAISANT LE SERVICE DE LA PLACE DE HAMBOURG (1813)

1813 Walking cuirassiers of the 1st Regiment serving at Hamburg Square

MAJOR DES ÉCLAIREURS
1814 Eclaireur major of young guards

1814 Hunter of the duke of Berry

1814 Voltgeur corporal with company guidon

1814-1815 Drums of the national guard of Paris

GARDE NATIONALE A CHEVAL DE PARIS (1ʳᵉ RESTAURATION)
(1814-1815)

1814-1815 National guard of Paris of 1st Restauration

1814-1815 King's Regt., 1st line infantry

OUVRIERS DE LA MARINE (1814-1815)

1804-1814 Honor guard of Lyon: general

1814-1815 Royal corps of French dragoons

CORPS ROYAL D'ARTILLERIE DE MARINE (1814-1825).
COMPAGNIE D'APPRENTIS CANONNIERS. — TAMBOUR, OFFICIER, SOUS-OFFICIER.

1814-1825 Royal navy artillery corps

LEGIONS DÉPARTEMENTALES. — CANONNIER DE LA 56ᵉ LÉGION (MOSELLE).

1815 Canonnier of the 56th legion (Moselle)

1815 Lieutenant of 15th hussar

GARDE NATIONALE A CHEVAL DE STRASBOURG
GUIDE DU GOUVERNEUR

1815 Strasbourg national guard at horse

1815 Uniform for the 8th Regt. of the royal guard

TIRAILLEUR FÉDÉRÉ
ou Voltigeur de la Garde Nationale Parisienne

1815 Voltigeur of Paris national guard

1815-1818 Carabinier and cuirassiers

1816 1st French infantry Regt. of the royal guard

1816 1st French infantry Regt. of the royal guard

1816 1st French infantry Regt. of the royal guard

1816 Northern hussars 4th Regt.

1816 Trumpets of the national guard on horse in Paris

CHASSEUR DE LA GUYANE
(1816-1823)

1816-1823 Guayane legion, chasseur

TAMBOUR DE GENDARMERIE (RESTAURATION).

1816-1830 Drum of the gendarmerie on foot

MARINE ROYALE (1816-1835)
Commis aux vivres.   Magasinier.

1816-1835 Royal navy

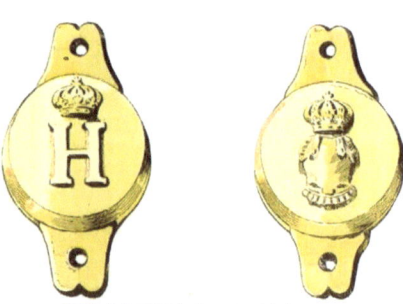

1850 Trumpet drapelle of guides at horse Regt. - 1830-1848 Horseback riding municipal guard gibern 1870 Belt tray of the foot chasseaur officers from legion of Antibes - 1820 Dragoon distinctive colors

TAMBOUR-MAJOR ET TAMBOUR-MAITRE D'INFANTERIE, GARDE ROYALE (1818).

1818 Royal guard infantry major and maitre drum

1818 Trumpet of the Garonne dragoons, 3rd Regt.

1818 Trumpet of the horse chasseaurs Regt. of Charente

ENSEIGNE DE VAISSEAU EN PETITE TENUE (1819-1835)

1819 Ship ensign

CHASSEUR D'INFANTERIE LÉGÈRE DES LÉGIONS DÉPARTEMENTALES
(1819-1820)

1819-1820 Light infantry chasseur of departmental legion

1820 Custom corps brigadier at horse

TROMPETTE MAJOR DE L'ARTILLERIE A CHEVAL DE LA GARDE ROYALE.

1820-1829 Trumpet-major of the royal guard horse artillery Regt.

CAPITAINE DE GRENADIERS DU 5ᵉ DE LIGNE

TENUE D'EXERCICE

1822 Grenadier officer of 5ᵗʰ line Regt.

GARDE - CHIOURME

1825 Garrison guard

1827 French officers and navy sailors

1828 Lancers' national guard on horseback from Mulhouse

1830 Swiss royal guard officer

**SECTION DU TRAIN DES ÉQUIPAGES
POUR LE SERVICE DE LA TRÉSORERIE DE L'ARMÉE
(EXPÉDITION D'ALGER 1830)**
1830 Train of equipage in Algerian campaign

OFFICIER DE ZOUAVES EN COSTUME ORIENTAL
(1830-1834)

1830-1834 Zouaves officer in oriental dress

TROMPETTE DU 2ᵉ CHASSEURS D'AFRIQUE (1832)

1832 Trumpet of the 2ⁿᵈ African chasseurs Regt.

OFFICIER DE CHASSEURS D'AFRIQUE
EN TENUE ORIENTALE

1832-1834 Officer of chasseur d'Afrique in oriental dress

1834 Custom corps: brigadier and private

CORPS DES DOUANES
BRIGADES A CHEVAL. — CAVALIER D'ORDRE

1835 Custom corps: brigadier at horse

1836 Ship officers navy post

1836 Navy saiolrs

1837 Fleet crew drum major

1837 Voltigeurs of the imperial guard

CORPS DES DROMADAIRES

Algérie (1843)

1843 Dromedary corps in Algery

CORPS DES DOUANES
CAVALIER D'ORDRE

1845 Custom corps: man at horse

1848 Drum major, chief of music and canteen director of the Paris mobile national guard

GARDE IMPÉRIALE (2ᵉ EMPIRE) DIVISION DU GÉNIE

1850 Engineers corps of imperial guard

9ᵉ HUSSARDS (1855).

1855 9th Hussars

J.-B. RENAULT, CHEF DE MUSIQUE DU RÉGIMENT D'ARTILLERIE A CHEVAL DE LA GARDE IMPÉRIALE (1855-1867).

1855-1867 Music chief of the horse artillery Regt. of the imperial guard

ESCADRON DES CENT GARDES (2ᵉ EMPIRE)
(Maréchal ferrant.)
(Cheval et harnachement de grande tenue.)

1857 Cent gardes squadron

1860 Veteran company

1864-1866 Colonel Dupin, commander of the French counter-guerrilla force in the Mexican campaign

1865 Cent gardes

CLAIRON ET CLAIRON MAJOR DE LA LÉGION D'ANTIBES OU ROMAINE (1866-1870).

1866-1870 Trumpeter and trumpeter major of the d'Antibes legion

LE PRINCE IMPÉRIAL EN TENUE DE FRANC-TIREUR DES VOSGES
(1867)

1867 The imperial prince in the uniforms of franc-tireurs of Vosges

ESCADRON DES ÉQUIPAGES MILITAIRES (2ᵉ EMPIRE)

Compagnies légères. — Mulet d'ambulance.

1870 Ambulance service 2ⁿᵈ empire

CHASSEUR A CHEVAL, 7ᵉ REGIMENT (1873)

1873 7ᵗʰ Regt. horse chasseur

CASQUE NOUVEAU MODÈLE POUR L'ARTILLERIE (1902).

1902 New model helmet for artillery

1830 French trumpet cavalry

1830 French colonial war

1818-1825 French grenadiers

1830 French war in north Afrika

1850-1850 French soldiers in the Champ of Chalon

1854 French army during the Crimean war

SOLDIERS, WEAPONS & UNIFORMS ALREADY PUBLISHED
(SOME TITLES)

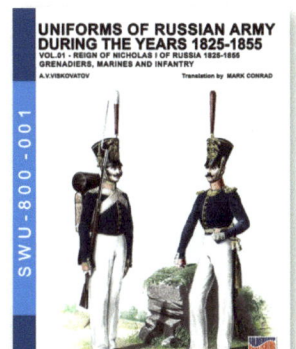
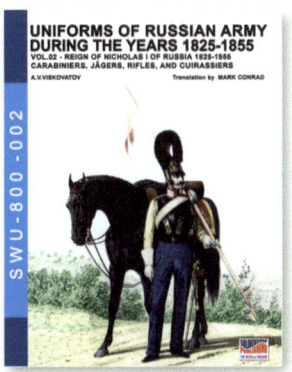
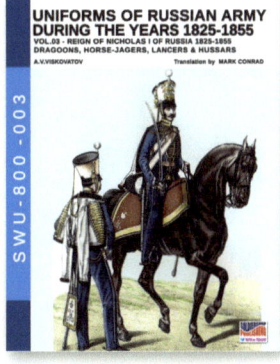
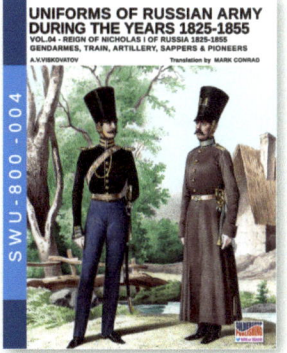
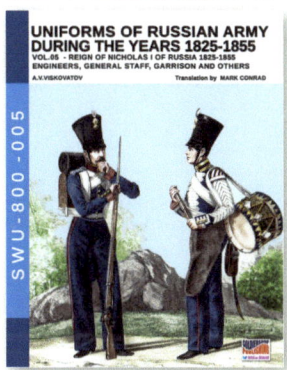
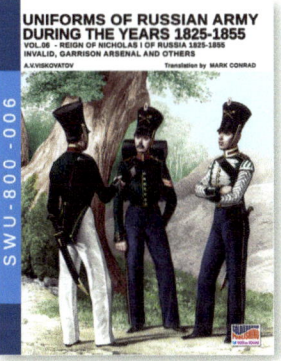
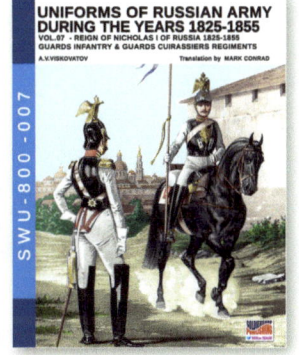

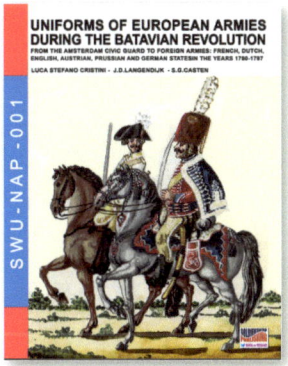
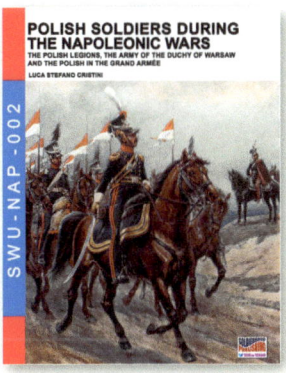

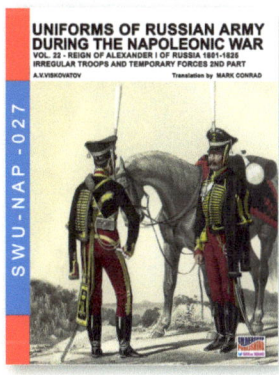

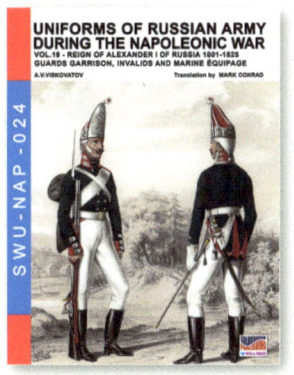

www.ingramcontent.com/pod-product-compliance
Lightning Source LLC
Chambersburg PA
CBHW041543220426
43664CB00003B/35